Published by Grolier Books, a division of Grolier
Enterprises Inc.

Disney Presents The Wonderful World of Knowledge
ISBN 0-7172-8929-X
Space ISBN 0-7172-8931-1

© 1999 Disney

First published in 1999

Printed and bound in China by
Toppan Printing Company

Originated in Italy by Articolor

Designed and compiled by
Marshall Editions Developments Limited

GROLIER
BOOKS

SPACE

Using The Wonderful World of Knowledge

Mickey, Minnie, Donald, Daisy, Goofy, and Pluto are ready to take you on an adventure ride through the world of learning. Discover the secrets of science, nature, our world, the past, and much more. Climb aboard and enjoy the ride.

Look here for a general summary of the theme

Labels tell you what's happening in the pictures

Mickey's ears lead you to one of the main topics

The pictures by themselves can tell you a lot, even before you read a word

Watch out for special pages where Mickey takes a close look at some key ideas

The Solar Syst

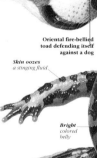

The Solar System is the given to our Sun and its fam planets. It also includes the moons, millions of pieces of called asteroids and meteor and frozen lumps of dust an called comets. Everything el can see in the sky is outside Solar System and is far, far away. Every single star is itself a sun, and each may have its own family of planets and moons.

Saturn is surrounded by beautiful rings

REPTILES AND AMPHIBIANS

Color and Camouflage

Frogs and toads come in nearly every imaginable color, even gold or black. They have a wide range of patterns, from spots and stripes to zigzags.

Color and pattern help frogs and toads survive. Bright colors warn that they may be poisonous. Drab colors camouflage them, or hide them against their background. Many tree frogs are exactly the same green as leaves, while others look like bark. The Asian horned toad has the best camouflage of all. Folds of patchy, brown skin and a flat body make it look like a dead leaf when it lies still on the forest floor.

Folds of brown skin give perfect camouflage

Flat body is hard to see among dead leaves

Asian horned toad

False-eyed frog

Markings look like eyes

For extra protection, bad-smelling liquid oozes out around false eyes

FALSE-EYED FROG
The South American false-eyed frog has large markings on its flanks that look like eyes. These fool some predators into thinking that they are looking at a much larger animal, such as a cat or bird.

COLOR AND CAMOUFLAGE

Dog sniffing curiously at the toad

Strawberry arrow frog

POISON-DART FROGS
Deadly poison oozes from the skin of Central and South American poison-dart frogs. People in the rain forest rub the tips of their arrows and blowpipe darts on the skin of these frogs to collect the poison to use for hunting.

Blue poison-dart frog

Oriental fire-bellied toad defending itself against a dog

Skin oozes a stinging fluid

Bright colored belly

Green and black back

FIRE-BELLIED TOAD
When cornered by a predator, the Oriental fire-bellied toad of eastern Asia arches its back and rears up on its legs to show its fiery underside. Wise attackers back off, because the toad's skin oozes a stinging, bad-tasting fluid.

Toad rears up on its back legs

FIND OUT MORE
MAMMALS: Camouflage
PLANET EARTH: Forests

16

17

Mickey's page numbers help you look things up. Don't forget there's a glossary and index at the back of each book

Goofy and his friends know how to give you a chuckle on every topic

Mickey points you to more information in other books in your *The Wonderful World of Knowledge*

FIND OUT MORE
MAMMALS: Camouflage
PLANET EARTH: Forests

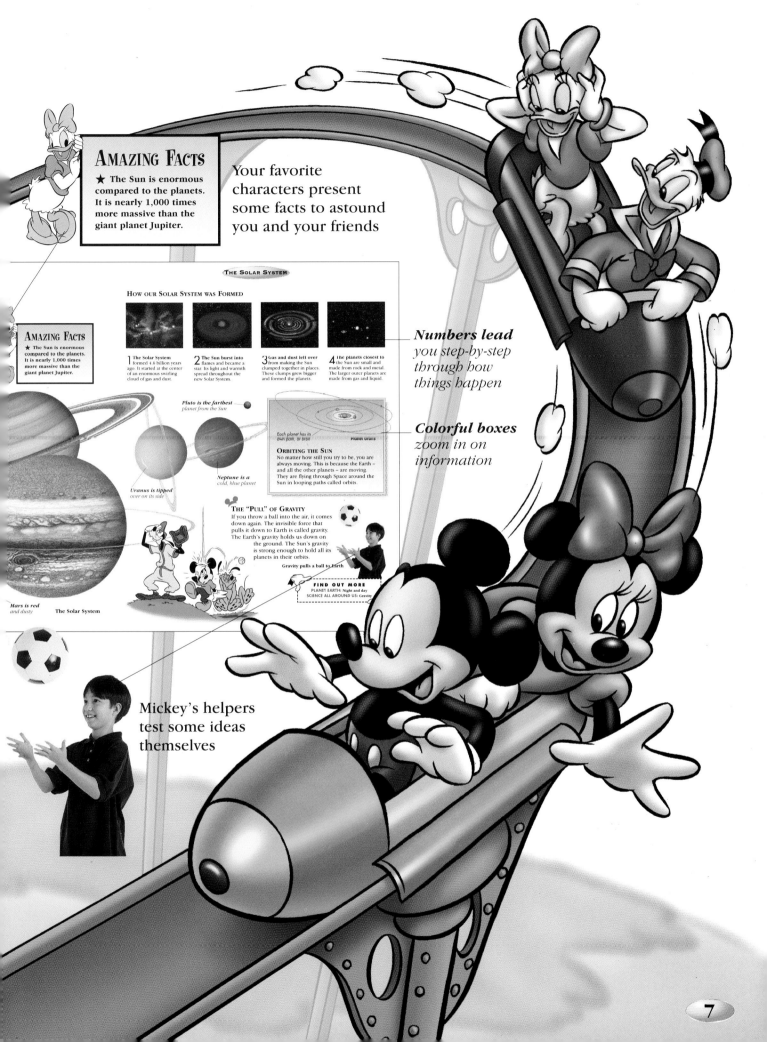

AMAZING FACTS
★ The Sun is enormous compared to the planets. It is nearly 1,000 times more massive than the giant planet Jupiter.

Your favorite characters present some facts to astound you and your friends

THE SOLAR SYSTEM

HOW OUR SOLAR SYSTEM WAS FORMED

1 The Solar System formed 4.6 billion years ago. It started at the center of an enormous swirling cloud of gas and dust.

2 The Sun burst into flames and became a star. Its light and warmth spread throughout the new Solar System.

3 Gas and dust left over from making the Sun clumped together in places. These clumps grew bigger and formed the planets.

4 The planets closest to the Sun are small and made from rock and metal. The larger outer planets are made from gas and liquid.

Numbers lead *you step-by-step through how things happen*

Pluto is the farthest planet from the Sun

Each planet has its own path, or orbit

Planet orbits

ORBITING THE SUN
No matter how still you try to be, you are always moving. This is because the Earth – and all the other planets – are moving. They are flying through Space around the Sun in looping paths called orbits.

Colorful boxes *zoom in on information*

Neptune is a cold, blue planet

Uranus is tipped over on its side

THE "PULL" OF GRAVITY
If you throw a ball into the air, it comes down again. The invisible force that pulls it down to Earth is called gravity. The Earth's gravity holds us down on the ground. The Sun's gravity is strong enough to hold all its planets in their orbits.

Gravity pulls a ball to Earth

FIND OUT MORE
PLANET EARTH: Night and day
SCIENCE ALL AROUND US: Gravity

Mars is red and dusty   **The Solar System**

Mickey's helpers test some ideas themselves

AMAZING FACTS
★ The Sun is enormous compared to the planets. It is nearly 1,000 times more massive than the giant planet Jupiter.

Contents

INTRODUCING
Space

Our planet, Earth, is just a speck in the vast, black ocean of Space. We have "neighbors": our Sun, our Moon, our fellow planets, and the flaming comets that race across our sky. But beyond are giant galaxies filled with billions of stars.

With space probes and amazing instruments, scientists are peering ever farther into the distance, and learning ever more about the nearer, twinkling spots we can see on a clear night. Will they ever find out where the mysterious darkness ends?

Looking into Space

👉 For thousands of years, people have been fascinated by the twinkling lights they saw in the night sky. Through the ages, astronomers studied the stars and planets and charted their movements. In time, they learned how to build instruments to look at the stars and to mark their positions. As they learned more about the stars and planets, their discoveries changed people's ideas about the Earth and its place in the whole Universe.

ARMILLARY SPHERE

Astronomers in Ancient China used armillary spheres to study the Moon and stars. As the Moon shines through the rings of the sphere, its position can be marked in the sky.

Armillary sphere built in 1744

FIRST TELESCOPE

The Italian Galileo Galilei (1564–1642) was the first astronomer to use a telescope to study the stars and planets. His observations showed that the Earth was not at the center of the Universe.

Galileo

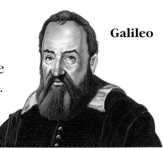

One of Galileo's first telescopes

Copernicus

Map of the Earth orbiting the Sun

AMAZING FACTS

★ Over 2,000 years ago Aristarchus of Ancient Greece suggested that the planets travel around the Sun. At the time, no one believed him.

COPERNICUS'S THEORY

Nicolaus Copernicus (1473–1543) was a Polish astronomer. In his day, the Christian Church taught that the Earth had been created at the center of the Universe. However, Copernicus believed that the Earth and planets moved around the Sun.

Binoculars make the Moon and stars look larger and closer than they look with just your eyes

There are billions of stars in the sky, but most are too faint to see

A small telescope reveals even more stars and smaller craters on the surface of the Moon

STAR-GAZING

If you look up into the sky on a clear night, well away from bright city lights, you will see hundreds of shining stars and the glowing Moon. If you have a good pair of binoculars or even a small telescope, you can see much, much more.

FIND OUT MORE
GREAT LIVES: Newton
STORY OF THE PAST: Astrolabe

The Solar System

The Solar System is the name given to our Sun and its family of planets. It also includes the planets' moons, millions of pieces of rock called asteroids and meteoroids, and frozen lumps of dust and gas called comets. Everything else you can see in the sky is outside the Solar System and is far, far away. Every single star is itself a sun, and each may have its own family of planets and moons.

AMADING FACTS

★ The Sun is enormous compared to the planets. It is nearly 1,000 times more massive than the giant planet Jupiter.

Saturn is surrounded by beautiful rings

THE SUN'S FAMILY

There are nine planets in the Solar System – from boiling Mercury, the closest planet to the Sun, to tiny Pluto, the most faraway world. All the planets have at least one moon, except for Mercury and Venus, which have none.

The Sun is a fiery hot star

Jupiter is a giant ball of liquid and gas

Mercury is the closest planet to the Sun

Venus is baking hot

Earth is our home planet

Mars is red and dusty

The Solar System

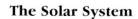

HOW OUR SOLAR SYSTEM WAS FORMED

1 **The Solar System** formed 4.6 billion years ago. It started at the center of an enormous swirling cloud of gas and dust.

2 **The Sun burst into** flames and became a star. Its light and warmth spread throughout the new Solar System.

3 **Gas and dust left over** from making the Sun clumped together in places. These clumps grew bigger and formed the planets.

4 **The planets closest to** the Sun are small and made from rock and metal. The larger outer planets are made from gas and liquid.

Pluto is the farthest *planet from the Sun*

Neptune is a *cold, blue planet*

Uranus is tipped *over on its side*

Each planet has its own path, or orbit

Planet orbits

ORBITING THE SUN

No matter how still you try to be, you are always moving. This is because the Earth – and all the other planets – are moving. They are flying through Space around the Sun in looping paths called orbits.

THE "PULL" OF GRAVITY

If you throw a ball into the air, it comes down again. The invisible force that pulls it down to Earth is called gravity. The Earth's gravity holds us down on the ground. The Sun's gravity is strong enough to hold all its planets in their orbits.

Gravity pulls a ball to Earth

FIND OUT MORE
PLANET EARTH: Night and day
SCIENCE ALL AROUND US: Gravity

The Sun, Our Star

The Sun looks bigger and brighter than any other star because it is so much closer to us. When the Sun rises each day, the sky fills with light and all the tiny twinkling stars seem to disappear from view until the Sun goes down again. Without the Sun's light and warmth, our Solar System would be a dark, cold place, and there would be no life on Earth.

SUN FACTFILE
Distance from Earth: 150 million km (93 million miles)
Diameter: 1.4 million km (865,000 miles)
Temperature: 6,000°C (10,800°F) at surface; 15 million°C (27 million°F) at center

The core is the hottest part of the Sun

Heat from the core spreads out in waves toward the surface

Prominences, or jets of gas, can be thousands of kilometers long

Photosphere, or Sun's surface

FLAMES OF FIRE
From Earth, the Sun looks like a peaceful yellow circle. But close up, its surface is a boiling, swirling sea of gas where huge explosions throw fiery flames deep into Space.

Sunspots are small dark patches on the surface of the Sun

AMAZING FACTS
★ The Sun is so far from Earth, a flight there by jumbo jet would take over 17 years.

ECLIPSE OF THE SUN

When the Moon passes between the Sun and the Earth, it casts a shadow on the Earth and blocks out the Sun's light for a few minutes. This is called an eclipse of the Sun, or a solar eclipse.

Why a solar eclipse happens

Earth

Moon

Sun

Sun's light

Partial solar eclipse
seen from the part of Earth partially in the Moon's shadow

Total solar eclipse
seen from the part of Earth totally in the Moon's shadow

GLOWING LIGHTS

Tiny particles stream from the Sun in all directions. When they fall into the Earth's atmosphere at the poles, they make a shimmering colored glow in the sky. We call them aurorae.

Aurora seen from Earth's North Pole

Never look directly at the Sun. Its light can damage your eyes.

Big prominences
may bend over into a loop

Close-up view of the Sun

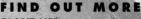

FIND OUT MORE
PLANT LIFE: Photosynthesis
SCIENCE ALL AROUND US: Light sources

Barren Mercury

Mercury is the closest planet to the Sun. It flies around the Sun very fast, so it is not pulled toward the Sun by the Sun's gravity. Mercury is a tiny world, not much bigger than the Moon. It has no atmosphere, or blanket of gases, to protect it, so it gets very hot and very cold. Its surface is bare and rocky, and it is covered with craters.

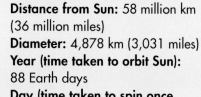

MERCURY FACTFILE
Distance from Sun: 58 million km (36 million miles)
Diameter: 4,878 km (3,031 miles)
Year (time taken to orbit Sun): 88 Earth days
Day (time taken to spin once on axis): 59 Earth days
Moons: 0

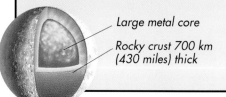

Large metal core
Rocky crust 700 km (430 miles) thick

ROCKS AND CRATERS
Mercury's craters were made when meteorites (large lumps of rock and iron) crashed into its surface.

Mercury is so close to the bright Sun that it is difficult to see from Earth

Craters and space rocks of all sizes litter Mercury's surface

The surface of Mercury

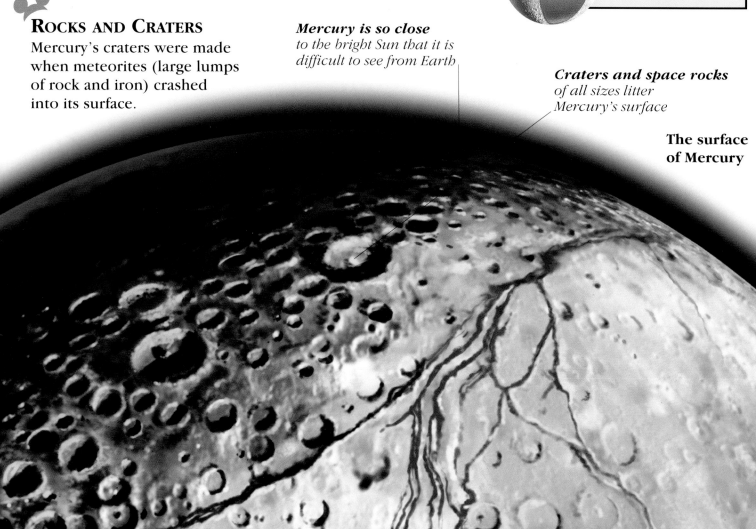

Mariner 10 flying toward the planet Mercury

AMAZING FACTS

★ A person would be nearly three times lighter in weight on Mercury than on Earth because Mercury has so little gravity.

Mercury with one side in darkness

HOT AND COLD

The side of Mercury facing the Sun is heated to 400°C (750°F) – four times hotter than boiling water and hot enough to melt lead. The temperature on the dark side of Mercury drops to a freezing –200°C (–330°F).

MARINER 10 PROBE

In the 1970s, a space probe called *Mariner 10* made history by being the first spacecraft to fly past two planets. It took the first pictures of Venus and sent them back to Earth by radio. It then traveled on to Mercury.

HOW A CRATER IS FORMED

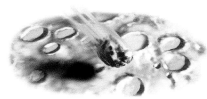

1 A meteorite crashes into a planet, throwing up huge clouds of rock and dust.

2 The rock and dust blast upward in all directions, then fall back down again.

3 The rock and dust settle in a wide circle around the dip made by the meteorite.

Mercury's surface will stay the same for millions of years because there is no wind or rain to disturb it

FIND OUT MORE
PLANET EARTH: Crater lakes
SCIENCE ALL AROUND US: Melting

Hot, Fiery Venus

Venus is the second planet from the Sun and, except for the Moon, it is our closest neighbor in Space. After the Sun and the Moon, it is the brightest thing you can see in the sky, especially just before sunrise and after sunset. Venus is almost the same size as the Earth, but it is a completely different world. Its surface is boiling hot, and its atmosphere is thick and poisonous.

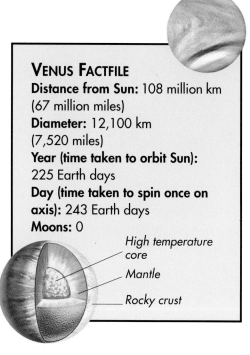

VENUS FACTFILE
Distance from Sun: 108 million km (67 million miles)
Diameter: 12,100 km (7,520 miles)
Year (time taken to orbit Sun): 225 Earth days
Day (time taken to spin once on axis): 243 Earth days
Moons: 0

High temperature core
Mantle
Rocky crust

VOLCANOES AND LAVA FLOWS

Erupting volcanoes send rivers of lava (molten rock) across Venus. The lava fills in most of the planet's craters. Because of this, Venus does not have as many craters as Mercury.

Volcano sends out lava

Landscape on Venus

Lava from volcanoes covers three-quarters of the planet's surface

CRUSHED BY CLOUDS

The first spacecraft that landed on Venus were destroyed by its crushing atmosphere. Later space probes, such as *Magellan*, used radar (radio signals) to "see" through the clouds and make maps of the planet.

Magellan made maps of the surface of Venus

Image of Venus's surface taken by *Magellan*

AMAZING FACTS

★ Venus's atmosphere blocks out blue light. Therefore, if you were standing on Venus, the sky would look red.

UNBREATHABLE AIR

Most of Venus's atmosphere is made from a gas called carbon dioxide. Chemical reactions between the atmosphere and the surface make clouds of choking sulfuric acid, which falls on the planet as acid rain.

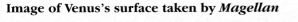

Ash and gas rising
from active volcano

Crater filled
in by lava

FIND OUT MORE
COMMUNICATIONS: Radio signals
PLANET EARTH: Volcanoes

Earth, Our Home

The Earth is special because it is our home. It is exactly the right distance from the Sun to receive just the right amount of light and heat. There is air to breathe, and there is plenty of water. These are essential for plants and animals to live. Earth is the only planet where we know for sure that life exists.

EARTH FACTFILE
Distance from Sun: 150 million km (93 million miles)
Diameter: 12,756 km (7,926 miles)
Year (time taken to orbit Sun): 365.26 days
Day (time taken to spin once on axis): 23.9 hours
Moons: 1

Solid metal inner core
Liquid metal outer core
Rocky mantle
Thin rocky crust

THE EARTH'S RICHES

The Earth has lush forests, grassy plains, high mountains, hot deserts, and freezing poles. Three-quarters of the planet is covered with water.

Mountains are the highest places on Earth

Oceans and seas cover most of the Earth's surface

The Earth's features

Flat plains are covered with trees, grass, and crops

Rivers provide fresh water

CHANGING SEASONS

The seasons are caused by the way the Earth is tilted on its axis. When the North Pole leans toward the Sun, it is summer in the northern half of the world and winter in the south. Six months later, it is winter in the north and summer in the south.

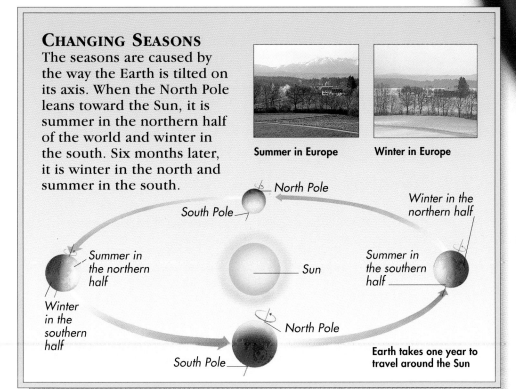

Summer in Europe

Winter in Europe

North Pole

South Pole

Winter in the northern half

Summer in the northern half

Sun

Summer in the southern half

Winter in the southern half

North Pole

South Pole

Earth takes one year to travel around the Sun

Earth's atmosphere

THE AIR WE BREATHE

The Earth's atmosphere, or air, is a mixture of gases – mainly oxygen and nitrogen. High in the atmosphere, there is less oxygen and nitrogen. The air gets thinner until it ends, and Space begins.

Why day and night happen

Axis

Day

Sun's light

Night

DAY AND NIGHT

The Earth spins once every 24 hours on an imaginary line called an axis. It is daytime on the side of the Earth that faces the Sun. On the opposite side, it is night.

Deserts are hot and dry with little rain

AMAZING FACTS

★ The Earth is spinning so fast that it carries someone standing on the Equator around Earth's middle a distance of 40,000 km (25,000 miles) in 24 hours, at a speed of 1,666 km/h (1,040 mph).

FIND OUT MORE
PLANET EARTH:
Deserts, Oceans

The Moon

The Moon is our closest neighbor in Space. It looks bright because it reflects light from the Sun. From day to day, the Moon seems to change shape. This is because, as it travels around the Earth, different parts of the Moon are lit up by the Sun's light. Unlike the Earth, the Moon has no air or life, and its surface is covered with craters.

AMAZING FACTS

★ The Moon spins once in the same time that it takes to orbit Earth. This means it always shows the same side, or face, to the Earth.

The Moon's surface

Earth seen *from the Moon*

MOON FACTFILE
Distance from Earth:
384,000 km (238,600 miles)
Diameter: 3,476 km
(2,160 miles)
Orbit (time taken to orbit Earth):
27 Earth days, 7 hours

THE MOON'S SEAS
If you look at the Moon, you can see large, dark areas on its surface. These patches are called seas, but they do not contain water. They are made from lava that flowed across the Moon's surface millions of years ago.

Some of the Moon's craters are more than 250 km (155 miles) wide

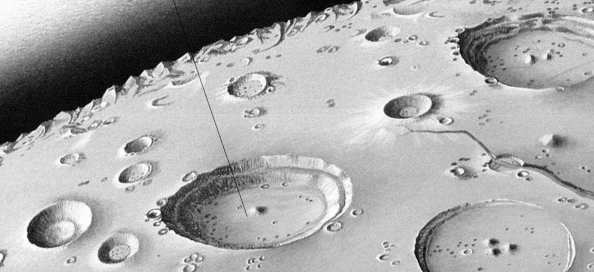

THE MOON'S CHANGING SHAPE

1 **A New Moon is** invisible from the Earth because the whole of the side facing the Earth is in the shade.

2 **A Crescent Moon** appears a couple of days later, when we can see one thin sunlit edge of the Moon.

3 **A Half Moon occurs** a few days after the Crescent Moon, when we can see half of the Moon's sunlit side.

4 **A Full Moon occurs** when the Moon has moved halfway around the Earth and we see the whole of its sunlit side.

ECLIPSE OF THE MOON

When the Earth passes between the Sun and the Moon, it casts a shadow on the Moon. People on the night side of the Earth see the Moon darken from a bright silvery circle to a dull red color as it enters the Earth's shadow.

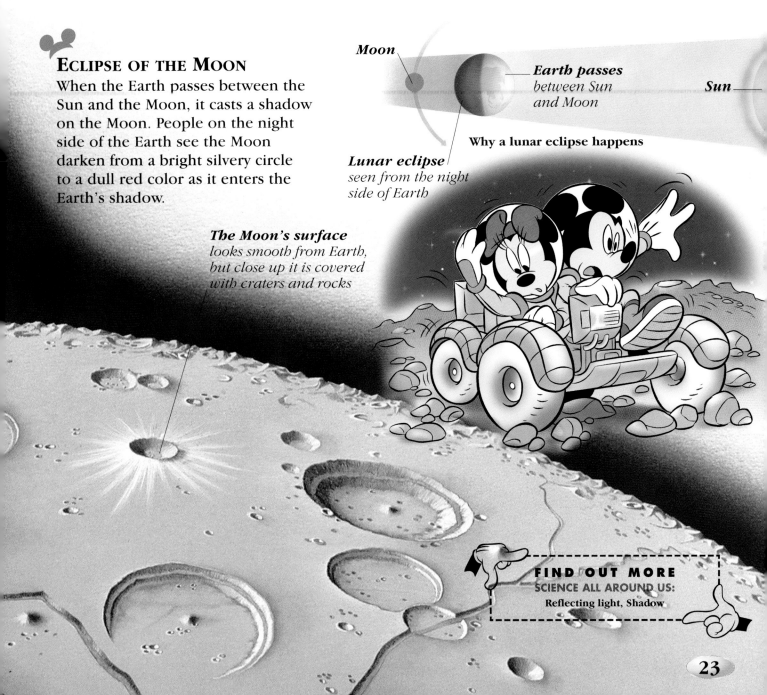

Moon

Earth passes
between Sun
and Moon

Sun

Why a lunar eclipse happens

Lunar eclipse
seen from the night
side of Earth

The Moon's surface
looks smooth from Earth,
but close up it is covered
with craters and rocks

FIND OUT MORE
SCIENCE ALL AROUND US:
Reflecting light, Shadow

Traveling into Space

We live in the space age. Astronauts fly into Space in space shuttles. Satellites circle the Earth. And tiny probes visit the distant planets.

Space is a dangerous place for people. Above Earth's atmosphere there is no air, and it is either boiling hot in the Sun or freezing cold in the shade. When people travel into Space, their spacecraft must protect them from the deadly heat and cold outside. It must also carry the air they need to breathe.

ROCKET POWER

Spacecraft are launched by rockets. Rockets are the only machines that are powerful enough to break away from Earth's gravity and fly into Space. The *Saturn V* rocket carried astronauts to the Moon.

Saturn V

Astronaut using an MMU (Manned Maneuvering Unit) to move around in Space

WALKING ON THE MOON

Twelve astronauts have walked on the Moon. Their footprints will still be there millions of years from now because there is no air to disturb them.

Trainee astronauts must get used to floating around weightless in Space

In July 1969, astronaut Neil Armstrong became the first person to walk on the Moon

SPACE-WALKING

Outside a spacecraft, astronauts wear a spacesuit to protect them. A spacesuit completely covers an astronaut's body, from head to toe. It keeps the astronaut from becoming too hot or too cold.

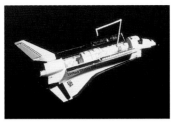

The Space Shuttle floating in Space

THE SPACE SHUTTLE

Rockets like *Saturn V* could only be used once, but the Space Shuttle can fly into Space again and again. It is often used to launch satellites. In 1990, it launched the Hubble Telescope.

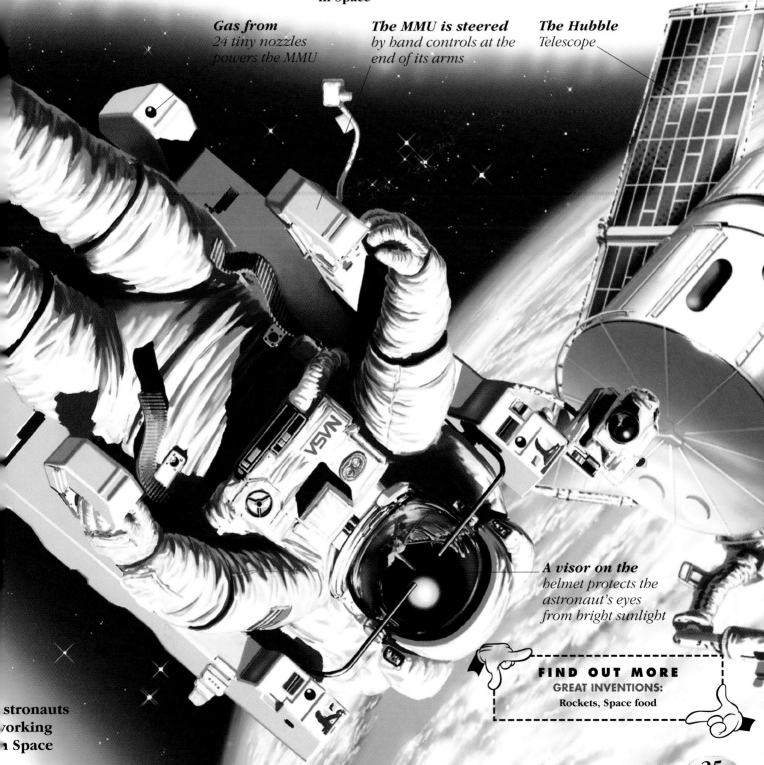

Gas from 24 tiny nozzles powers the MMU

The MMU is steered by hand controls at the end of its arms

The Hubble Telescope

A visor on the helmet protects the astronaut's eyes from bright sunlight

Astronauts working in Space

FIND OUT MORE
GREAT INVENTIONS:
Rockets, Space food

Red and Rocky Mars

Mars is a cold, rocky planet. It is also known as the Red Planet because it is covered with rust-red dust. Strong winds often blow the dust about the planet in huge storms. Mars has seasons like the Earth, but it is much colder because it is farther from the Sun.

MARS FACTFILE
Distance from Sun: 228 million km (142 million miles)
Diameter: 6,786 km (4,217 miles)
Year (time taken to orbit Sun): 687 Earth days
Day (time taken to spin once on axis): 24.6 Earth hours
Moons: 2

Solid metal core
Mantle
Rocky crust

CRATERS AND VOLCANOES
Mars is covered with craters, just like the Earth's Moon. But on Mars the craters are worn away by the wind and dust storms. The volcanoes on Mars look like those on the Earth, but they are much bigger.

Pathfinder **spacecraft on the surface of Mars**

Red dust blown *about by strong winds*

Pathfinder *sent pictures of Mars back to Earth*

Dried-up river bed *where water may once have flowed across the planet*

THE MOONS OF MARS

Mars has two moons,
Phobos and Deimos.
They are both small and
pitted with craters. They
are strange shapes, too –
they look a little like giant
potatoes. Phobos is 25 km
(15 miles) across. Deimos
is 13 km (8 miles) across.

AMAZING FACTS

★ The biggest volcano on
Mars, Olympus Mons, is
26 km (16 miles) high –
that means it is three
times higher than Earth's
tallest mountain, Everest.

Olympus Mons

Everest

THE QUESTION OF LIFE

The *Pathfinder* spacecraft landed
on Mars in 1997. It sent pictures of
the red, rocky surface of Mars back
to Earth. However, it did not find
any signs of life.

**Close-up views of the
surface of Mars show
red rocks and dust**

Craters show
where meteorites fell
millions of years ago

FIND OUT MORE
FAMOUS PLACES: Mount Everest
INSIDE MACHINES: Remote vehicles

Giant Jupiter

Jupiter is by far the biggest of all the planets in the Solar System. It is 10 times bigger than the Earth. Jupiter is not made of rock like the Earth. It is made of the same gases as the Sun, but it never grew big enough to become a star itself. Clouds swirl around Jupiter in colorful bands of red, yellow, and white, and storms on its surface can rage for hundreds of years.

Jupiter's features

The Great Red Spot is a storm 40,000 km (24,840 miles) across – three times the size of Earth

Dark areas are hotter, deeper layers of gas seen through gaps in clouds

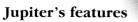

JUPITER FACTFILE
Distance from the Sun:
778 million km (484 million miles)
Diameter: 142,984 km
(88,846 miles)
Year (time taken to orbit Sun):
11.9 Earth years
Day (time taken to spin once on axis): 10 Earth hours
Moons: 16

Hydrogen and helium gases

Tiny rocky core

Faint ring of dust particles

Heavier hydrogen gas

GAS GIANT
Jupiter is called a gas giant because it has no solid surface like the Earth. Instead, its tiny rocky core is surrounded by a thick blanket of gases. These gases are mainly hydrogen and helium.

Ganymede

JUPITER'S MOONS
Jupiter has 16 moons. The four largest – Io, Europa, Ganymede, and Callisto – are all bigger than the planet Pluto. Ganymede is the biggest moon in the Solar System. These four moons are known as the Galilean moons because they were discovered by the astronomer Galileo Galilei in 1610.

Io is a hot moon *with constantly erupting volcanoes*

Freezing cold Europa *is covered with fresh ice, smooth enough to skate on*

Sulfur lava from active volcano

VOLCANOES ON IO

Io is the closest moon to Jupiter. In 1979, the two *Voyager* space probes took photographs of its erupting volcanoes.

Io is covered by reddish sulfur

FIND OUT MORE
PLANET EARTH:
Clouds, Storms

Ringed Saturn

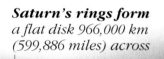 **S**aturn is the second-largest planet in the Solar System. It looks different from all the other planets because it is surrounded by broad, flat rings. Although other planets have rings, none are as clear or as beautiful as Saturn's. Like Jupiter, Saturn is a gas giant. It is made up mainly of two gases called hydrogen and helium.

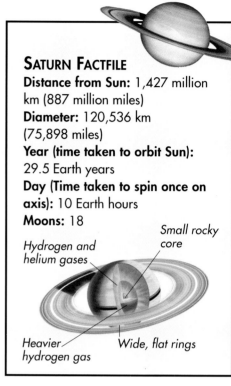

SATURN FACTFILE
Distance from Sun: 1,427 million km (887 million miles)
Diameter: 120,536 km (75,898 miles)
Year (time taken to orbit Sun): 29.5 Earth years
Day (Time taken to spin once on axis): 10 Earth hours
Moons: 18

Hydrogen and helium gases

Small rocky core

Heavier hydrogen gas

Wide, flat rings

Saturn's rings form a flat disk 966,000 km (599,886 miles) across

Clouds of gas swirl around Saturn's small metal core

A BEAUTIFUL PLANET

From Earth, Saturn looks like a bright golden star in the sky. With a small telescope, it is possible to see Saturn's rings and at least four of its moons.

The rings are thin, so if you look at them edge-on they almost disappear

Saturn

Saturn's outer moons are balls of icy rock

SATURN'S MOONS

Saturn's 18 moons are freezing cold worlds because of their great distance from the Sun. The largest of them, Titan, is the only one with an atmosphere.

Phoebe

Tethys

AMAZING FACTS

★ When Galileo discovered Saturn in 1610, his telescope was not powerful enough to show the rings clearly. He thought the bulges on the sides of the planet were moons, and he wrote that "Saturn has ears."

Enceladus

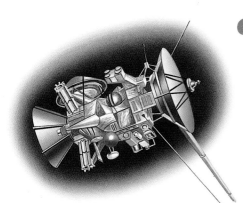

CASSINI PROBE

In 1997, the *Cassini-Huygens* spacecraft was launched on its way to Saturn. When it reaches the planet in 2004, the *Huygens* part of the probe will land on Titan. The *Cassini* craft will go on to orbit Saturn.

Mimas

Cassini-Huygens space probe

SWIRLING RINGS

From Earth, it looks as if Saturn has three broad rings. Close-up views from space probes show that there are actually lots of rings. Each ring is made up of millions of bits of rock and ice, all swirling around Saturn in their own orbits.

Titan, the largest of Saturn's moons

Saturn's rings are made up of chunks of rock and ice

FIND OUT MORE
GREAT LIVES: Galileo
SCIENCE ALL AROUND US: Ice

31

Uranus, Neptune, and Pluto

☞The planets farthest from the Sun, also called the outer worlds, are Uranus, Neptune, and Pluto. Uranus and Neptune are roughly the same size – about 4 times the size of Earth. Both have thick atmospheres, small rocky cores, and faint rings. Pluto is much smaller than the Earth. It is so far away that it is very difficult to spot, even with a very strong telescope.

Uranus's dark rings were only discovered 20 years ago by the Voyager *space probes*

Uranus is tipped over on its side

URANUS FACTFILE
Distance from Sun: 2,871 million km (1,784 million miles)
Diameter: 51,118 km (31,763 miles)
Year (time taken to orbit Sun): 84 Earth years
Day (time taken to spin once on axis): 17.24 Earth hours
Moons: 17

Faint rings made from small dark particles

Hydrogen gas with methane clouds

Heavier hydrogen gas

Small rocky core

THE OUTER WORLDS
Uranus and Neptune are gas giants like Jupiter and Saturn, but not as big. Pluto is a small ball of icy rock. It is so far from the Sun that it has a very wide orbit.

Uranus

AMAZING FACTS

★ Since Pluto was discovered in 1930, it has traveled only one quarter of its wide orbit around the Sun.

PLUTO AND CHARON

We know very little about Pluto and its single moon, Charon, because they are so far away. Charon was only discovered in 1978. It is half the size of Pluto.

Neptune's Great Dark Spot is a storm the size of the Earth

Pluto

Neptune

Fast winds race across Neptune's surface at 2,000 km/h (1,250 mph)

Voyager probe

PLUTO FACTFILE
Distance from Sun: 5,914 million km (3,675 million miles)
Diameter: 2,284 km (1,419 miles)
Year (time taken to orbit Sun): 249 Earth years
Day (time taken to spin once on axis): 6.4 Earth days
Moons: 1

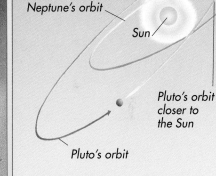

Neptune's orbit

Sun

Pluto's orbit closer to the Sun

Pluto's orbit

THE FARTHEST PLANET
Pluto is usually the farthest planet from the Sun. However, for part of its orbit it actually swings closer to the Sun than Neptune. During this time, therefore, Neptune is the most distant planet.

VOYAGER PROBES
In the 1970s and 1980s, two space probes, *Voyager 1* and *Voyager 2*, took the first close-up photographs of the Outer Worlds.

NEPTUNE FACTFILE
Distance from Sun: 4,497 million km (2,794 million miles)
Diameter: 49,528 km (30,775 miles)
Year (time taken to orbit Sun): 165 Earth years
Day (time taken to spin once on axis): 16.1 Earth hours
Moons: 8

FIND OUT MORE
PLANET EARTH: Rock
SCIENCE ALL AROUND US: Gas

Space Through Telescopes

Astronomers look into Space through powerful telescopes to learn more about how the Universe was formed and to search for signs of life on other worlds.

Light and radio waves arrive at the Earth all the time from distant parts of the Universe. Optical telescopes have lenses or mirrors and use light waves to study the stars. Radio telescopes have large dishes or aerials to pick up radio waves. Some scientists are looking for radio signals that may have been sent by beings from another world.

Scientists use special machines to listen for signals from Space at SETI (Search for Extraterrestrial Intelligence) Institute

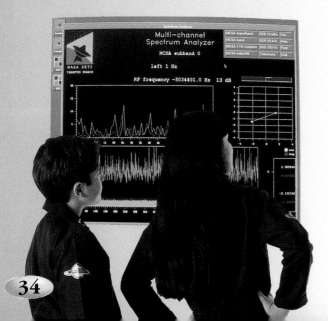

EYES IN SPACE

The Hubble Space Telescope produces sharp and clear photographs of distant stars. It sends them back to Earth by radio signals.

Hubble Space Telescope

Radio telescope

RADIO TELESCOPES

Radio telescopes, such as the Very Large Array Telescope in New Mexico, use large dishes to pick up radio signals from Space.

A door in the dome slides open to let starlight into the telescope

ABOVE THE CLOUDS

The swirling air around the Earth bends starlight. This makes it hard for astronomers to study the stars. To solve this problem, big optical telescopes are built on top of high mountains, where the air is thinner and cleaner.

Starlight enters
the telescope here

Secondary mirror
reflects light from main
mirror into eyepiece
(below main mirror)

Stars stand out clearly
against the black sky
in the thin, clean air

**Mountain-top
optical telescope**

IS ANYONE THERE?

A message was sent into Space in
1974 from the Arecibo radio
telescope in Puerto Rico. It may
reach another star – and other
kinds of intelligent life – in the
year 27,000.

Message is
"scrambled" and
includes information
about people,
counting, and
telescopes

Main mirror
(behind frame) focuses
light, making faraway
stars seem closer

Strong steel frame
holds the mirror steady

Arecibo message

FIND OUT MORE
COMMUNICATIONS: Satellites
GREAT INVENTIONS: Lenses

Asteroids and Meteoroids

☞ **A**steroids are ancient pieces of rock left over from when the planets were made. Millions still travel around the Sun. Meteoroids are smaller pieces of rock and dust. Some of them reach Earth, but they burn up in the atmosphere because they are so tiny. If a meteoroid reaches the ground, it is called a meteorite.

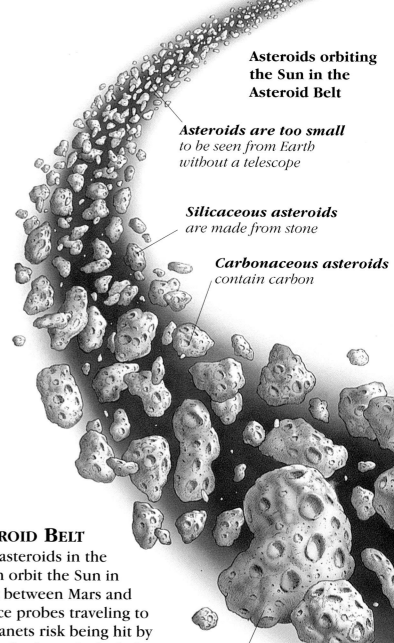

Asteroids orbiting the Sun in the Asteroid Belt

Asteroids are too small to be seen from Earth without a telescope

Silicaceous asteroids are made from stone

Carbonaceous asteroids contain carbon

THE ASTEROID BELT
Most of the asteroids in the Solar System orbit the Sun in a broad belt between Mars and Jupiter. Space probes traveling to the outer planets risk being hit by them as they fly through the belt.

Metallic asteroids contain iron

Asteroids break up into smaller pieces when they collide

COLLIDING ASTEROIDS
Big asteroids sometimes crash into each other and break up into smaller pieces. Millions of years ago there were probably just a few hundred asteroids that collided again and again.

AMAZING FACTS
★ The largest-known asteroid in the Asteroid Belt is called Ceres. It is 1,000 km (600 miles) across.

★ Most meteors are tiny bits of dust left behind from a comet's tail.

WISH UPON A STAR

When a meteoroid enters the Earth's atmosphere, it heats up so much that it glows, making a bright streak in the night sky. We call these streaks of light meteors, or shooting stars.

Some people like to make a wish when they see a shooting star

BARRINGER CRATER

About 50,000 years ago, a meteorite about 60 m (200 ft) across smashed into Arizona, U.S.. It produced a crater 175 m (575 ft) deep and 1,265 m (4,150 ft) wide.

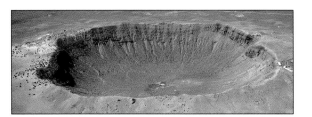

Barringer crater

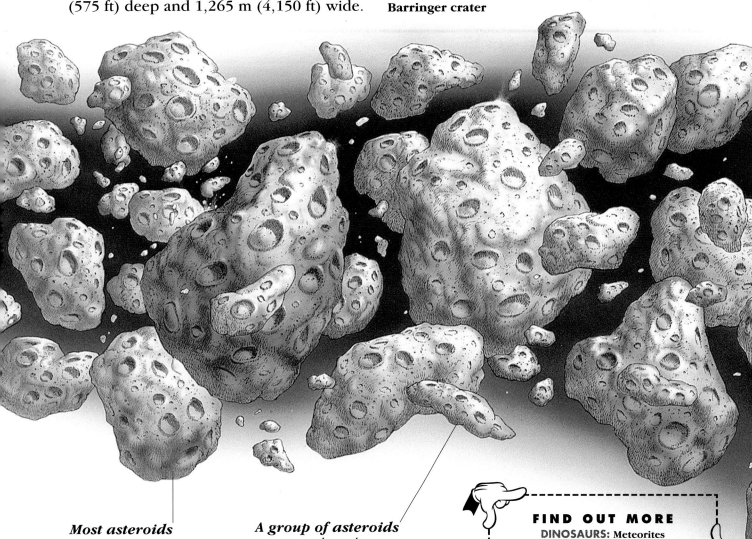

Most asteroids *are as old as the Solar System itself*

A group of asteroids *may once have been one large asteroid that broke up*

FIND OUT MORE
DINOSAURS: Meteorites

37

Flaming Comets

Comets are chunks of rock and ice a few kilometers wide. Most comets are far away in the outer parts of the Solar System. But some have long looping orbits that bring them close enough to the Sun for us to see them. A comet looks like a bright streak or smudge in the sky. Some have glowing tails millions of kilometers long.

AMAZING FACTS

★ Some of the biggest comets ever seen have had tails 160 million km (100 million miles) long. That's more than the distance between the Earth and the Sun.

A GLOWING TAIL

A comet's tail is made of dust and gas, which streams behind the comet as it nears the Sun. It looks like a glowing, hot flame, but it is really freezing cold. It only glows because it reflects sunlight.

Comet with tail trailing behind it

Nucleus is made of rock, dust, and ice

Coma is a cloud of gas and dust surrounding the nucleus

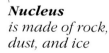

HOW A COMET BEGINS

1 When a comet is about as far from the Sun's warmth as the planet Mars, it starts giving off gas.

2 As it nears the Sun, gas and dust pour from the comet in a glowing cloud called the coma.

3 Tiny particles streaming from the Sun sweep the gas and dust into a long tail.

From Earth, the tail
looks like a milky smudge

Dust tail streams
behind the comet's head

Gas tail
points away
from the Sun

Comet West

TWO-TAILED COMET

Some comets, such as Comet West, have two tails pointing in quite different directions. In these comets, the faint blue gas tail points away from the Sun. The white or yellow dust tail, made of heavier particles, trails back in the direction the comet has come from.

HALLEY'S COMET

Halley's comet was named after the English astronomer Edmund Halley. In 1705, Halley correctly predicted that a comet he had seen in 1682 would return every 76 years or so – and it did.

Halley's comet shown on the Bayeux Tapestry in 1066

Halley's comet seen in 1986

FIND OUT MORE
SCIENCE ALL AROUND US: Particles

39

Star Maps

The stars seem to change their position in the sky from night to night and through the year. This is because the Earth spins as it travels around the Sun. Maps of the sky show the stars divided into 88 groups, called constellations. These maps will help you to find some of the groups.

To use the star maps, first find the right map for the right month. It shows the constellations as they appear in the evening (9:45p.m. standard time) looking south. If you live north of the Equator, you will mostly see the constellations shown in the top half of the map. If you live south of the Equator, you will mostly see the ones shown in the bottom half, so turn the book upside down to use the map.

Can you find some of the constellations?

OLDEST STAR MAP

The oldest existing star map in the world comes from Ancient China. It is about 900 years old.

Chinese star map

JUNE TO NOVEMBER

The blue star Vega can be seen overhead from the northern half of the Earth and part of the southern half. See if you can spot the square Pegasus constellation, or the bright star Fomalhaut near Capricornus.

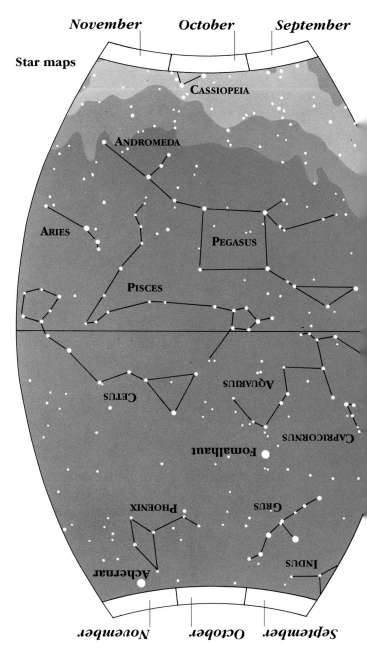

November   *October*   *September*

Star maps

CASSIOPEIA

ANDROMEDA

ARIES

PEGASUS

PISCES

CETUS

AQUARIUS

CAPRICORNUS

Fomalhaut

GRUS

PHOENIX

INDUS

Achernar

November   *October*   *September*

Map of constellations
over the North Pole

NORTH POLE STAR

If the movement of the stars were speeded up, they would appear to move around one fixed point in the sky. In the northern sky, the closest star to this fixed point is Polaris, the Pole Star.

STAR MAGNITUDE

The brightness of stars as seen from Earth is measured on the magnitude scale. The brightest stars are magnitude 0 or -1. We can see stars up to about magnitude 6 with the naked eye.

-1
0
1
2
3
4

Stars move from east to west through the year, so read the months from right to left

Libra – meaning "scales" – is one of the 12 constellations making up the signs of the zodiac

Our Solar System is part of the Milky Way galaxy, which can sometimes be seen as a band of faint, pale starlight stretching across the sky

Near the Equator, you can see stars from both halves of the map

FIND OUT MORE
ATLAS OF THE WORLD:
Equator, North Pole

Patterns in the Sky

From ancient times, people have told stories about the stars and the patterns they make in the sky. People have also used the stars to navigate, or find their way.

Travelers in the northern half of the Earth could find the direction of the North Pole by looking for Polaris, the Pole Star. Travelers in the southern half could find the direction of the South Pole by looking for the four stars in the constellation Crux, the Southern Cross. Once they knew which direction was north or south, they knew the other directions, too. Early travelers could cross an ocean or find their way across a desert by using the stars in this way.

STAR GODS

The Mayan people of Central America believed their gods sometimes took the form of the stars and planets.

Mayan picture-writing showing gods as planets

DECEMBER TO MAY

Look out for the three bright stars which make up Orion's "belt." You may also be able to see the bright dog star, Sirius, or the constellation of Leo, the lion.

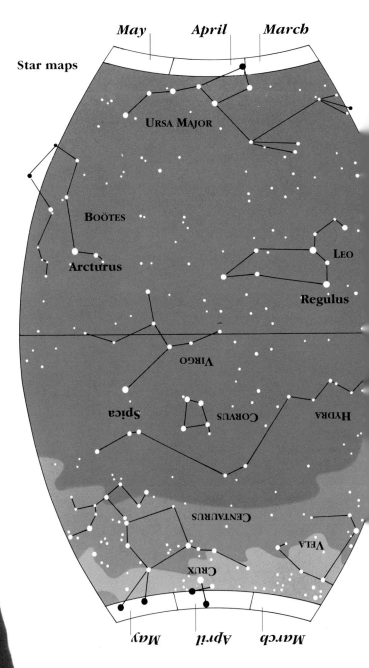

Star maps

May   April   March

URSA MAJOR

BOÖTES

Arcturus

LEO

Regulus

VIRGO

Spica   CORVUS   HYDRA

CENTAURUS

VELA

CRUX

May   April   March

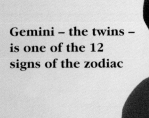

Gemini – the twins – is one of the 12 signs of the zodiac

SOUTH POLE STARS

There is no star exactly at the sky's South Pole. The closest stars to the South Pole form the cross-shaped constellation Crux, the Southern Cross.

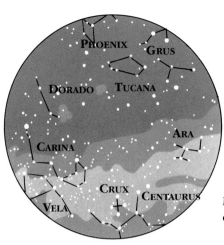

Map of constellations over the South Pole

STAR OR PLANET?

Stars and planets look similar in the night sky, but there are two ways to tell them apart. First, the planets shine steadily, but stars seem to twinkle. Second, the planets slowly move in relation to the stars.

Twinkling starlight

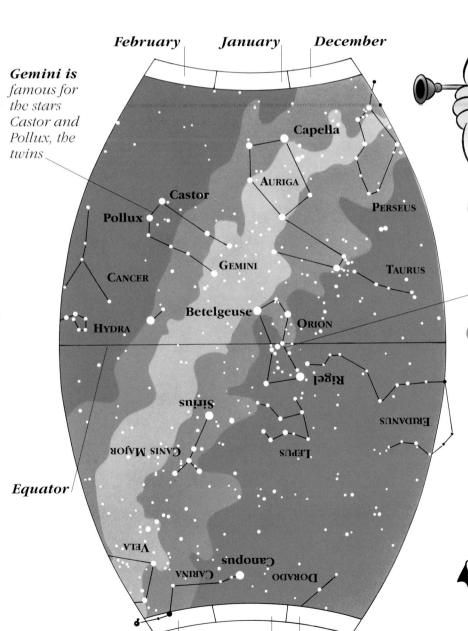

Gemini is famous for the stars Castor and Pollux, the twins

February January December

Capella

AURIGA

Castor

Pollux

PERSEUS

Gemini

TAURUS

CANCER

Betelgeuse

ORION

HYDRA

Rigel

Sirius

CANIS MAJOR

LEPUS

ERIDANUS

Equator

VELA

Canopus

CARINA

DORADO

February January December

PHOENIX GRUS

DORADO TUCANA

ARA

CARINA

CRUX CENTAURUS

VELA

Orion, the hunter, with a belt of three bright stars

SIGNS OF THE ZODIAC

Every year, the Sun passes through the same 12 constellations. These make up the signs of the zodiac. Most of the signs are animals, such as Taurus, the bull, and Cancer, the crab.

Cancer

FIND OUT MORE
COMMUNICATIONS: Mayan codices
TRAVELERS AND EXPLORERS: Navigation

The Life of a Star

A star begins its life in a cloud of gas and dust called a nebula. New stars are forming and old stars are dying all the time, so there are stars of all ages in the Universe. An average star shines for billions of years. Our own star, the Sun, is about 5 billion years old – halfway through its life.

1 **New stars form** from clumps of gas and dust inside a nebula.

A STAR IS BORN

A nebula provides all the raw material needed to create new stars. Clumps of hydrogen gas and dust shrink, pulled inward by their own gravity. As they shrink, they heat up and finally burst into light.

AMAZING FACTS

★ In about 5 billion years, the Sun will swell up and become a red giant. It will become 100 times bigger than it is now. The Earth will be heated to thousands of degrees and will finally spiral into the center of the Sun.

2 **Some of the** gas shrinks and forms a spinning ball.

STAR COLORS

Astronomers can tell how hot a star is by looking at its color. The hottest stars burn faster than the coolest stars and don't live as long.

 White stars are about 10,000°C (18,000°F)

 Yellow stars, like our Sun, are about 6,000°C (10,800°F)

 Blue stars are the hottest, at about 40,000°C (72,000°F)

 Orange and red stars are the coolest, at about 3,000°C to 4,500°C (5,400°F to 8,100°F)

6 Finally, the star cools and slowly fades into a black dwarf.

5 Eventually, the red giant uses up all its remaning fuel. It then shrinks and becomes a white dwarf.

4 When the star has used up most of its hydrogen fuel, it swells up into a red giant and burns lower-grade fuel.

The red giant star, Betelgeuse

A RED GIANT

A star shines as it uses up its fuel, or hydrogen gas. When it has used up most of its gas, it swells up, turns orange or red and becomes a "red giant."

3 The shrinking ball of gas heats up and becomes a star. A medium-sized star shines for about 10 billion years.

FIND OUT MORE
SCIENCE ALL AROUND US: Heat

Supernovae and Neutron Stars

A medium-sized star like our Sun will eventually become a red giant then shrink into a white dwarf. But a much bigger star will swell into a red supergiant then – instead of shrinking – will blow itself up in a huge explosion called a supernova. All that is left is the star's small spinning center, called a neutron star. Neutron stars, or pulsars, send beams of radio waves out into Space.

A SUPERNOVA EXPLOSION
When a star explodes, it can shine as brightly as 10 billion Suns – but not for long. It fades over the next few weeks or months until it is so faint that it almost disappears from view.

CRAB NEBULA
In the year 1054, people reported an unusually bright star in the sky. In fact, it was a supernova explosion. The cloud of gas and dust blasted into Space can still be seen today. It is called the Crab nebula. New stars may be forming inside the nebula.

Crab nebula

A supernova explosion

Neutron star

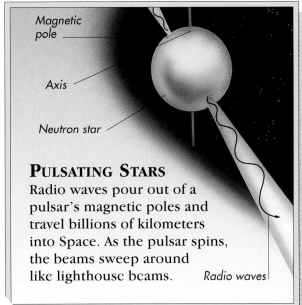

Magnetic pole

Axis

Neutron star

Radio waves

PULSATING STARS
Radio waves pour out of a pulsar's magnetic poles and travel billions of kilometers into Space. As the pulsar spins, the beams sweep around like lighthouse beams.

PICKING UP PULSARS
If a pulsar's radio waves sweep across the Earth, they can be picked up by a radio telescope. They produce a series of blips, or pulses, that can be seen on a graph.

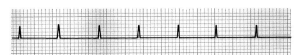

Regular blips from a pulsar

AMAZING FACTS
★ Supernovae are so bright that at least five of them were seen with the naked eye, before the invention of the telescope.

FIND OUT MORE
SCIENCE ALL AROUND US:
Radio waves

Black Holes

When really massive stars die, they turn into the strangest things in the Universe – black holes. A black hole has such an incredibly strong force of gravity nothing can escape from it, not even light! Although black holes are invisible, their gravity reaches far into Space. This gravity pulls things toward it, such as gases from a nearby star. To find a black hole, astronomers look for the effect of its gravity.

Black hole

A SHRINKING STAR
The size of a star shrinks greatly when it becomes a black hole. If our Sun were to become a black hole, its existing diameter of 1.4 million km (865,000 miles) would be shrunk to a diameter of just 6 km (4 miles).

Dust and gas spiral into a black hole

AMAZING FACTS

★ Quasars are the most distant known objects in the whole Universe. They produce huge amounts of energy, but no one really knows what they are.

LOOKING FOR BLACK HOLES
Dust and gas from a nearby star heat up as they are pulled toward a black hole. As they heat up, they give out light, radio waves, and X-rays. Astronomers use special satellites to scan the sky for X-rays and find black holes.

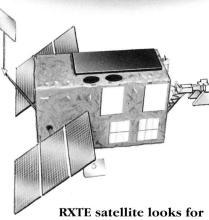

RXTE satellite looks for black holes

Gas from a nearby *star is pulled toward the black hole*

A BLACK HEART

Strange objects called quasars may have huge black holes at their centers. Quasars look like stars, but they are so far away they must be as bright as billions of stars.

Quasar

Stars, gas, and *dust swirl around a black hole at the center of a quasar*

Jets of gas *escape from the quasar along the axis of the disk*

Black *hole*

Event *horizon*

Dust and gas

Black Hole

FALLING INTO A BLACK HOLE

The area around a black hole from which nothing can escape is called the event horizon. Anything inside the event horizon could be sucked into the black hole by its gravity and lost from the Universe forever.

FIND OUT MORE
GREAT INVENTIONS: First satellite
INSIDE MACHINES: X-rays

The Milky Way

☞ Our star, the Sun, is part of an enormous group, or galaxy, of stars called the Milky Way. The Milky Way contains 200 billion stars in the shape of a giant spiral. If you look up on a clear night, well away from city lights, you may see the Milky Way as a faint band of milky white light stretching across the sky.

From Space, the Milky Way looks like a huge spiral of stars

Dust and gas hide the hub, or center, of the galaxy from view

MEASURING IN LIGHT-YEARS

Galaxies are so huge and so far apart that scientists need a special way of measuring them – in light-years. A light-year is the distance that light travels in one year. That is 10 trillion km (6 trillion miles). Our galaxy, the Milky Way, is a staggering 150,000 light-years across and 1,500 light-years thick.

The Milky Way

AMAZING FACTS

★ If you could travel at the speed of light, it would take 28,000 years to reach the center of the Milky Way from the Earth.

★ The Moon is about one light-second away from the Earth. The Sun is 8 light-minutes from the Earth.

DIFFERENT GALAXIES

Galaxies are divided into different types by their shape. Most are spiral or elliptical. Some spirals have a bar across the middle. Irregular galaxies have no particular shape.

Spiral galaxy

Barred spiral galaxy

Elliptical (egg-shaped) galaxy

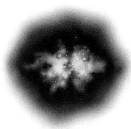

Irregular galaxy

Globular, or round, clusters of stars contain up to a million stars

Spiral arms of stars curl around the galaxy

The Andromeda galaxy – the closest large galaxy to the Milky Way

ANDROMEDA GALAXY

The Andromeda galaxy, also known as M31, is a beautiful spiral galaxy like the Milky Way. It contains about 300 billion stars and is 2.4 million light-years away. It can just be seen with the naked eye from Earth.

The Local Group

The Local Supercluster

BEYOND THE MILKY WAY

The Milky Way and about 30 other galaxies move through Space together in a cluster called the Local Group. These clusters in turn clump together to form superclusters. The Local Group is part of the Local Supercluster.

FIND OUT MORE
SCIENCE ALL AROUND US:
Light paths

The Big Bang

The history of the Universe

The Universe began with a huge explosion called the Big Bang

☞**M**ost scientists now think that the whole Universe began about 15 billion years ago in a huge explosion called the Big Bang. At that time, all material in the Universe was squeezed into a tiny point. Then the Universe burst out in all directions. At first it was very hot, but as it expanded, it cooled. The Universe is still expanding and cooling today.

The ball of energy made by the explosion expanded and began to cool

EXPANDING UNIVERSE

The tremendous force of the Big Bang is still pushing the galaxies apart. Test this out for yourself. Draw some galaxies all over a balloon. This represents the Universe. Now blow up your balloon Universe and see how the galaxies move apart.

THE FIRST ATOMS

When the Universe was four minutes old, scientists believe it had cooled enough for tiny particles to join together and form the first atoms. Atoms are the building blocks of everything in the Universe.

Hydrogen – the first atom (shown millions of times larger than actual size)

The galaxies move farther apart as the balloon is inflated

Galaxies in Space

LOOKING BACK IN TIME

The most distant galaxies are so far away that light from them takes billions of years to reach us. When scientists look at them, therefore, they see the galaxies as they were billions of years ago.

The first particles
of matter formed

The first stars
and galaxies formed from vast clouds of gas

The galaxies
are still moving apart

MAPPING THE UNIVERSE

In 1992, the COBE satellite produced a microwave map of the sky showing a faint glow. This glow is the remaining energy from the Big Bang itself. The hotter areas are pink and red. These show where gases, then galaxies, first started to form.

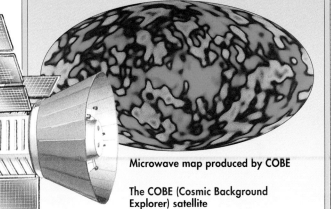

Microwave map produced by COBE

The COBE (Cosmic Background Explorer) satellite

AMAZING FACTS

★ The Universe may go on expanding forever or it may stop expanding and shrink again. If it shrinks, it will end in a Big Crunch.

★ A Big Crunch could be the Big Bang that starts a new Universe.

FIND OUT MORE
COMMUNICATIONS: Microwaves

The Future in Space

Space travel has only just begun, but changes are happening very fast. In the future, we may even be able to live on distant planets.

Many people all over the world are excited by space travel and what may be found far, far away in Space. That is why television programs and science fiction movies about spaceships and traveling to different parts of the Universe are so popular. Who knows? Perhaps one day, you will be able to travel to the Moon or even visit Mars.

SPACE IN MOVIES
If you enjoy watching science fiction movies, there are plenty to choose from. Hundreds of movies have been made about space travel and meeting creatures from other planets.

Scene from the movie
E.T. The Extra-Terrestrial

Mining on the Moon

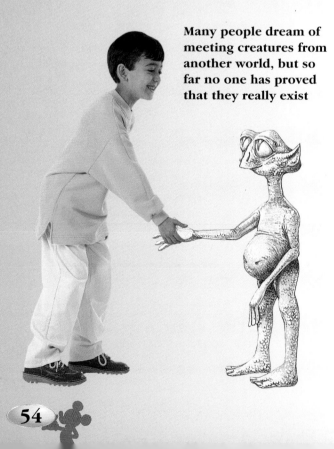

Many people dream of meeting creatures from another world, but so far no one has proved that they really exist

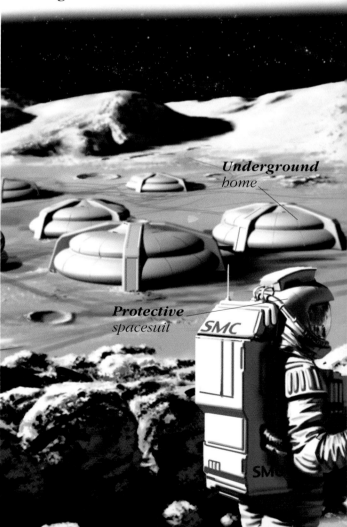

Underground home

Protective spacesuit

SMC

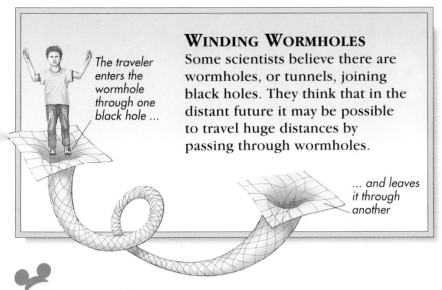

WINDING WORMHOLES
The traveler enters the wormhole through one black hole ...

Some scientists believe there are wormholes, or tunnels, joining black holes. They think that in the distant future it may be possible to travel huge distances by passing through wormholes.

... and leaves it through another

SPACE STATION FREEDOM
The United States, Japan, Russia, and several other countries are working together to build a space station that will orbit Earth. Astronauts and scientists will be able to live and work there.

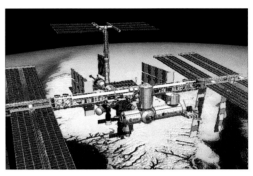

Artist's picture of Space Station Freedom

MINING IN SPACE
Some asteroids are rich in metals. Just one of them could supply all the iron we need on Earth. In future, asteroids may be moved to the Moon so that they can be mined more easily.

Lunar mining equipment

Asteroids mined for valuable metals

Lunar car

FIND OUT MORE
INSIDE MACHINES:
Digging machines

Glossary of Key Words

Asteroid: A piece of rock in orbit around the Sun. An asteroid may be as small as a grain of sand or up to 1,000 km (621 miles) wide.

Astronomer: A scientist who studies moving objects in Space.

Atmosphere: The gas that surrounds a star, planet, or moon.

Aurorae: The colored lights seen in the sky at the Earth's poles.

Axis: An imaginary line running from pole to pole through the middle of a spinning star, planet, or moon.

Black dwarf: The final stage a star goes through as it dies.

Black hole: An object created by the collapse of a huge star. Its force of gravity is so powerful that nothing, not even light, can escape.

Carbon dioxide: A gas that has no color or smell, and which is present in the atmospheres of many planets.

Coma: The cloud of gas and dust surrounding a comet.

Comet: A lump of dust and ice in orbit around the Sun.

Constellation: A group of stars that make a shape in the sky when they are seen from the Earth.

Crater: A large hole made when a meteorite crashes into the surface of a planet or moon.

Crust: The rocky surface layer of a planet or moon.

Elliptical: Shaped like a squashed circle. Moons and planets often move in elliptical orbits.

Galaxy: A collection of billions of stars moving through Space.

Gravity: The force that pulls everything toward the center of a star, planet, or moon.

Helium: A lightweight, colorless gas found inside stars.

Hydrogen: The lightest gas, and the most common substance found inside stars.

Lens: A piece of glass or clear plastic, shaped so that it bends light rays as they pass through.

Light waves: Electromagnetic (electric and magnetic) vibrations that our eyes can detect. We see light waves of different lengths as different colors. Light waves travel through Space at a speed of 300,000 km (186,300 miles) per second.

Light-year: The distance that light travels in one year. Often used as a unit of measurement for really large distances.

Magnitude: In astronomy, a number describing the brightness of a star. The larger the number, the fainter the star appears to be.

Mantle: The deep, heavy rock inside a planet on which the thin surface crust floats.

Meteorite: A meteoroid that reaches the ground, often forming a crater.

Meteoroid: A piece of rock that travels through Space and enters the Earth's atmosphere, forming a glowing shooting star, or meteor.

Moon: A natural satellite orbiting a planet, and the name given to the Earth's only natural satellite.

Nebula: A cloud of gas and dust in Space. Some nebulae glow brightly while others are dark.

Nitrogen: A gas that makes up four-fifths of the air around us.

Orbit: The path of a planet as it travels around a star, or of a satellite as it travels around a planet.

Oxygen: A gas that makes up just over one-fifth of the air around us and is essential for most life.

Prominence: A jet of gas that shoots out from the Sun's surface.

Pulsar: A pulsating star that sends out radio waves.

Quasar: Quasar stands for quasi-stellar object, or QSO. It means something that looks like a star but is not a star. No one knows exactly what quasars are, but they may be bright, distant galaxies.

Radio signal: A beam of radio waves that carries information.

Radio waves: Electromagnetic vibrations that carry radio signals through Space.

Satellite: An object that moves around another, usually a planet. It can be a natural satellite, such as a moon, or an artificial satellite, such as a spacecraft.

Solar System: The Sun, the nine planets and their moons, comets, asteroids, and everything else that orbits the Sun.

Star: A giant, glowing ball of gas, such as the Sun.

Supernova: A star that explodes and, for a few years, shines as brightly as a whole galaxy of stars.

Universe: All the space, matter, and energy that exists everywhere.

White dwarf: A small, faint star about 1,000 km (621 miles) across, produced when a star the size of the Sun has used up all its fuel and collapses.

Index

*(see **Famous Places** for a full index to your complete set of books)*